ERIC CLAPTON FOR THE CLASSICAL GUITAR

Arranged by John Zaradin.

Wise Publications
London/New York/Sydney

Exclusive Distributors:
Music Sales Limited
8/9 Frith Street, London, W1V 5TZ, England
Music Sales Pty. Limited
120 Rothschild Avenue, Rosebery, NSW 2018, Australia

This book © Copyright 1992 by
Wise Publications
Order No. AM88272
ISBN 0-7119-2935-1

Designed by Pearce Marchbank Studio
Music arranged & processed by John Zaradin

Music Sales complete catalogue lists thousands of
titles and is free from your local music shop, or direct from Music Sales Limited.
Please send a cheque/postal order for £1.50 for postage to:
Music Sales Limited, Newmarket Road, Bury St Edmunds, Suffolk IP33 3YB.

Your Guarantee of Quality
As publishers, we strive to produce every book to the highest
commercial standards.
The music has been freshly engraved and the book has been carefully
designed to minimise awkward page turns and to make playing from it
a real pleasure.
Particular care has been given to specifying acid-free,
neutral-sized paper which has not been elemental chlorine bleached but produced
with special regard for the environment. Throughout, the printing
and binding have been planned to ensure a sturdy, attractive
publication which should give years of enjoyment.
If your copy fails to meet our high standards, please inform us
and we will gladly replace it.

PRESENCE OF THE LORD
Words & Music by Eric Clapton

4

5

WONDERFUL TONIGHT
Words & Music by Eric Clapton

8

HELLO OLD FRIEND
Words & Music by Eric Clapton

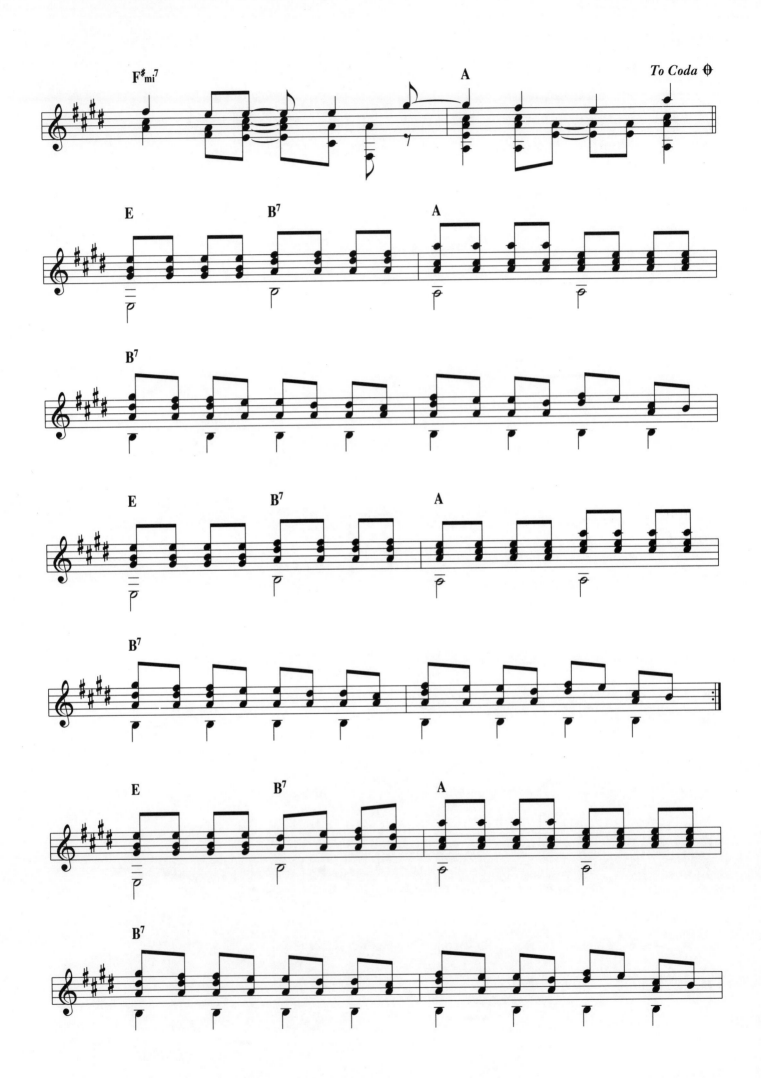

I SHOT THE SHERIFF
Words & Music by Bob Marley

D.S. al Coda

LET IT GROW
Words & Music by Eric Clapton

BETTER MAKE IT THROUGH TODAY
Words & Music by Eric Clapton

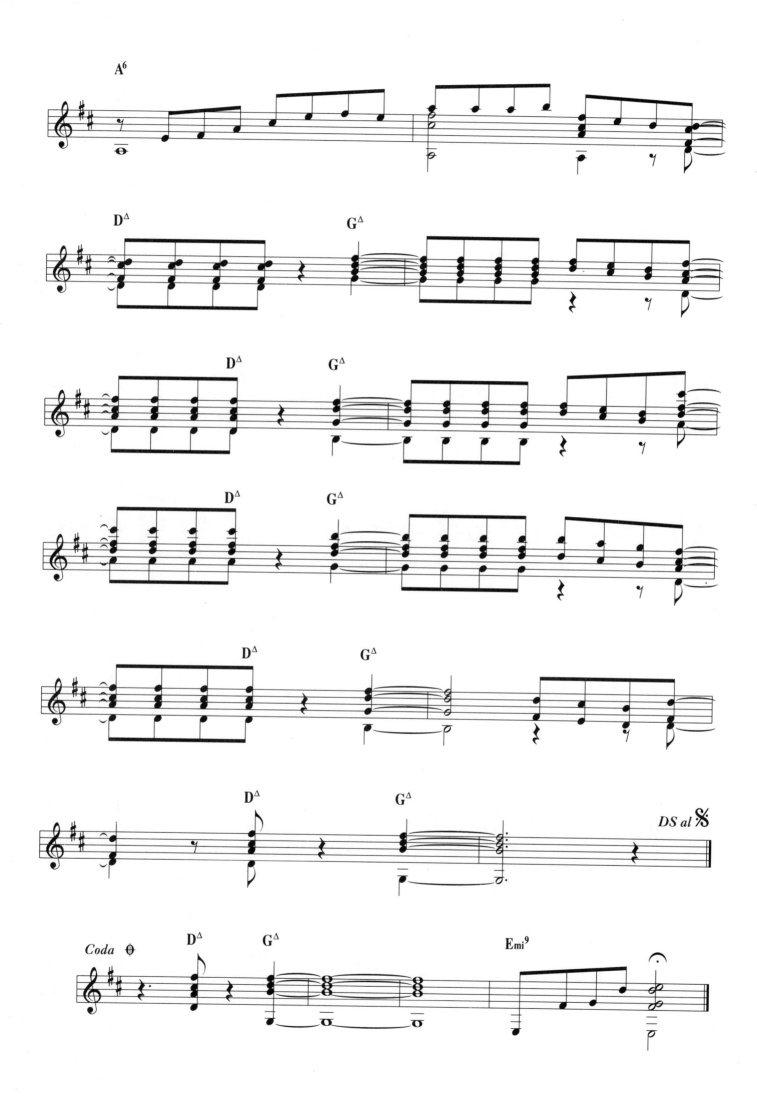

SUNSHINE OF YOUR LOVE
Words & Music by Jack Bruce, Pete Brown
& Eric Clapton

28

THE SHAPE YOU'RE IN
Words & Music by Eric Clapton

Bright Blues Shuffle

LAYLA
Words & Music by Eric Clapton & Jim Gordon

LAY DOWN SALLY
Words & Music by Eric Clapton, Marcy Levy
& George Terry

Walking bass throughout

Introduction

45

repeat & ad lib fade

Printed in Great Britain by
Printwise (Haverhill) Limited, Haverhill, Suffolk   6/97 (27977)

Notes to The Music in This Volume

This collection of songs by Eric Clapton is new repertoire for the
classical guitar and introduces solo adaptations of the music that
are not simply score reductions of the originals.

Where the music is dependent on the amplification or sound effects
of the electric, steel-strung guitar, I have made modification to
it, or created new passages, that are more idiomatic of the
acoustic, fingerstyle instrument.

Examples are found:
a) in the solos and improvisations, which sometimes extend beyond
the fingerboard range of the classical guitar.
b) where to maintain a continuity of the bass and solo lines
produces an impossible or uncharacteristic solo part.
c) where a section is left open for improvising.
d) where a part is intended to be played by another instrument,
such as keyboards.

Chord symbols are included for reference to denote the basic
background harmonies.

My intention in arranging these very popular songs has been to
produce musically satisfying pieces that the classical guitarist
can add to his repertoire both for study and performance.

John Zaradin, London 1992.

ERIC CLAPTON FOLIOS AVAILABLE FROM MUSIC SALES…

THE ERIC CLAPTON ANTHOLOGY 1

EIGHTEEN SONGS IN GUITAR TABLATURE AND STANDARD
NOTATION, WITH LYRICS AND CHORD SYMBOLS.
ORDER No. AM83502

THE ERIC CLAPTON ANTHOLOGY 2

GUITAR TABLATURE AND STANDARD NOTATION,
WITH LYRICS AND CHORD SYMBOLS.
ORDER No. AM83569

ERIC CLAPTON ROCK SCORE 1

NOTE-FOR-NOTE SCORE FOR PROFESSIONAL
AND SEMI-PROFESSIONAL GROUPS.
ORDER No. AM83551

ERIC CLAPTON ROCK SCORE 2

NOTE-FOR-NOTE SCORE FOR PROFESSIONAL
AND SEMI-PROFESSIONAL GROUPS.
ORDER No. AM83577

CREAM ROCK SCORE

NOTE-FOR-NOTE SCORE FOR PROFESSIONAL
AND SEMI-PROFESSIONAL GROUPS.
ORDER No. AM83585

ERIC CLAPTON: STRANGE BREW

ELEVEN SONGS IN GUITAR TABLATURE AND STANDARD
NOTATION, WITH LYRICS AND CHORD SYMBOLS.
ORDER No. AM83536

ERIC CLAPTON: BLUES POWER

NINE SONGS IN GUITAR TABLATURE AND STANDARD
NOTATION, WITH LYRICS AND CHORD SYMBOLS.
ORDER No. AM83528

DEREK AND THE DOMINOS:
LAYLA AND OTHER ASSORTED LOVE SONGS

MATCHING FOLIO IN PIANO/VOCAL ARRANGEMENTS,
WITH LYRICS AND SPECIAL GUITAR NOTATION.
ORDER No. AM83296

ERIC CLAPTON

PIANO/VOCAL ARRANGEMENTS WITH SPECIAL
GUITAR TABLATURE SECTION.
ORDER No. AM14739

THE COMPLETE GUITAR PLAYER
ERIC CLAPTON SONGBOOK

INCLUDES RHYTHM PATTERNS IN TABLATURE AND
LEFT-HAND FINGERINGS, PLUS LYRICS AND CHORD BOXES.
ORDER No. AM83593